The Cats History
Western of Art

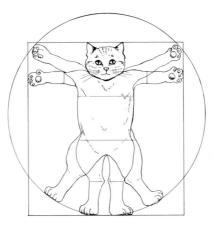

The Cats History
Western of Art

SUSAN HERBERT

WITH COMMENTARIES BY
GENEVIEVE McCAHEN

With 31 colour illustrations

THAMES AND HUDSON

FRONTISPIECE

Delacroix's study for
Greece Expiring in the Ruins of Missalonghi.

❖

© 1994 Thames and Hudson Ltd, London
Reprinted 1994

British Library Cataloguing-in-Publication Data
A catalogue record for this book is available from the British Library

ISBN 0-500-01610-0

Printed and bound in Singapore by C.S. Graphics

Editor's Preface

❖

Art historians have been universally puzzled by the recent discovery that many painters, sculptors, watercolourists, printmakers – throughout the ages – have used cats as models in the preliminary sketches they made for some of their greatest and most beloved masterpieces. The scholars of our breed have made valiant attempts to produce various explanations for this unexpected and rather bizarre phenomenon, but none of the theories advanced so far have been at all convincing. No doubt the main problem is that the practice appears to have been so widespread, ranging from the early Egyptians to those artists of our own day who indulge in realism rather than abstraction. As research continues, further evidence may yet be forthcoming, along with more compelling explications.

To my own way of thinking, explanations are quite unnecessary. Let us simply assume that most artists have been fond of cats, and in many (if not all) historical phases and places – think of Rembrandt's Amsterdam in the early 17th century, for instance – no self-respecting establishment could survive without the feline element to keep down the rodent population. After all, the Pied Piper of Hamlin could not be everywhere at once. In addition, it has occurred to me that the very expressionlessness of cats presents the artist with a specific and useful problem: how to make a point about an individual without recourse to such human facial arrangements as smiles, scowls, frowns or pouts. Whatever the reasons for all these cat-works, our good fortune is that they represent a kind of history of art. That is how I present them here, in the hope that this rather light-hearted approach to a serious subject may be helpful in the learning process.

Associate Professor Genevieve McCahen
UNIVERSITY OF CATALINA ISLAND

❖

The earliest example of an artist using a cat as a model is this remarkably well preserved papyrus sketch for Tutankhamun's coffin, which I discovered in an obscure corner of the burial chamber in 1973. Dare I suggest that, with her last purr, it was this cat who placed the famous curse upon the tomb?

❖

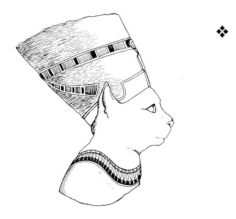

Susan Herbert.

❖

The 6th-century BC Greek potter Exekias was devoted to his cats. In fact I have conclusively identified several forged Exekiases by the absence of tiny cat hairs embedded in the clay. The model for Achilles, in this study for a scene from the Trojan Wars, was Oedipuss, one of Exekias's favourites. He was renowned for his willingness to pose for hours while wearing uncomfortable armour.

Kitachthonios, Exekias's most melodramatic model, here plays Penthesilea, the dying Queen of the Amazons.

❖

❖

This Roman Fresco, of about the 1st century BC, was discovered by chance after the removal of an outer layer of paint. The artist is anonymous and there is no way of verifying whether he or she used cats as models for this scene of Venus chastising Cupid. However, the awkward angle at which Cupid's wings jut out has led me to conclude that the artist almost certainly tied a set of imitation wings to a real cat.

❖

❖

The Byzantine Age is noted for its brilliant mosaics. Since it is unlikely that the Empress Theodora would have posed for a mosaic, it is far more reasonable to speculate that the artist used a feline stand-in.
Given Theodora's rather fearsome reputation, one wonders if he wasn't taking a considerable risk in depicting her as a cat – though to a cat-lover the resemblance could only be seen as complimentary. Theodora's particular interest in animals, as described by the historian Procopius in his scurrilous *Secret History*, did not extend to cats.

❖

❖

I t is with Gothic art that the use of cats as models acquires a function of greater significance than mere convenience. As other scholars have noted, one of the major developments of the art of the 15th century was a more flexible and natural style of representation. Since cats are far more flexible and natural than humans, it was inevitable that artists would first practise this development on their cats. It took the three Limbourg brothers over three years to create the *Très Riches Heures* for the Duc de Berry because they fought constantly among themselves over whose cat was to play which part in the studies for their illuminations.

❖

❖

The Flemish painter Jan van Eyck was one of the first portraitists in oil. It is easy to imagine how useful cat models are to the portrait painter, for it takes many studies and many sittings to get the likeness just right. For this portrait of his wife, however, it was the subject, not the painter, who enlisted the help of Eyckstasy, the family cat. Van Eyck had developed several disagreeable work habits, frequently grinding his teeth and cleaning his ears with the sharp wooden end of his paintbrushes.

Finally, after many hours of forbearance, Mrs Van Eyck insisted that her husband use the cat to work out the technical difficulties of the portrait to spare her. The famous look of wary resignation, which both the cat and human portraits share, is no doubt due to Van Eyck's unfortunate behaviour.

❖

❖

It seems unlikely that Bellini would have been able to pay so much attention to the details of dress in his portrait of the Doge Leonardo Loredan if it had been inhabited throughout the entire sitting by the Doge himself. Bellini's cat would have made a far more patient and entertaining model.

❖

SUSAN HERBERT

With Botticelli we come to the early Renaissance in Florence. One of the great achievements of Renaissance art was the mastery with which painters were able to employ large numbers of cats in the same sitting. As any cat-lover knows, persuading several cats to co-operate with you as well as each other is a demanding task and this study for *Spring* (*Primavera*) is the first great painting to use the technique successfully. Other important technical advances are evident. Notice, for instance, how much more assuredly the wings on the blindfolded Cupid at the top of the painting have been tied to the kitten when compared with the earlier Roman fresco.

❖

❖

Titian was not only a follower of Bellini, he cared for Bellini's cats after the artist's death. I have positively identified the cat in this study for Titian's painting of a young man as the very same one who, as a kitten, posed for a number of studies by Bellini.

❖

T V

Susan Herbert

❖

L eonardo da Vinci was of course the great genius of the Renaissance. Though he used cats as models, his scientific interest led him to experiment with them further. Many scholars have remarked on the luminous depth and soft fluid darkness of Leonardo's painting, yet I am the first to demonstrate how Leonardo achieved these effects. Before the paint had dried, he would hold a cat up to the canvas and, while stroking it, would 'finish' the surface with its gently twitching tail.

❖

Susan L Herbert

With Michelangelo, the supreme technical development of Renaissance art is fully realized: the effective use of large numbers of cats as study models. Michelangelo regarded his studies for larger works as so important, that his version of the birth of Adam for the Sistine Chapel was delayed for several months to await the birth of an entire litter of kittens who were to become the models for the Lord's wingless angels. Michelangelo's ability to organize a litter of eight kittens to pose for many days is truly a masterly accomplishment.

Susan Herbert

❖

Raphael actually disliked cats. But he was a great rival of Michelangelo and, upon learning that Michelangelo had employed Pope Julius's cats for his studies for the Sistine Chapel, he proposed to Pope Leo X that he use Leo's cats for this study. The ploy was successful, and Raphael enjoyed considerable patronage from Leo.

❖

Here we see that painters of the Flemish Renaissance were also adept at peopling their paintings with many cats. This is one of the very few cat studies by Pieter Bruegel the Elder. His son, Pieter the Younger, was allergic to cats and the Elder Bruegel was thus forced to give all the cats away shortly after his son's birth. A distinct falling off in the quality of Bruegel's art can be noticed from this time on.

❖

This self-portrait of Rubens seated next to his wife raises one of the most significant questions in the use of cat models – why? Obviously, when an artist paints a self-portrait, there is no need of a cat as a model, since the artist can use a mirror (except in the case of those extremely rare artists who are unable to look at themselves for very long). However, for this painting, Rubens' wife was disinclined to pose for hours beside a mirror. Her diary records this charming exchange:
'I would prefer, my dear, to sit next to you!'
'You shall, my dearest. Let us employ the family cats.'

❖
_____

Rembrandt's difficult personality caused him to offend his patrons and lose many important portrait commissions. It was his son Titus, finally, who persuaded him to use cats for the early sittings for this portrait, *The Syndics of the Clothmakers' Guild.* Cats, as we know, are extremely sensitive to their owners' moods, and in the baleful expressions of his cats Rembrandt saw reflected his own attitude to his subjects. Here the ability of felines to give an artist insight into the creative process could truly be called catalytic.

❖

35

This is one of the most significant works of all studies with cats. By using only his beloved Siamese (a notoriously narcissistic breed) to model a painting whose subject is narcissism, Velázquez has added a dimension to this version that even the final painting does not possess.

❖

Vermeer, whose self-conscious sense of interior space seems to reach out to include the viewer, here self-consciously employs a cat to model the artist, himself.

❖

This work by Van Dyck is altogether unique in the annals of cat studies, for it is a study for a study for a bust of King Charles I of England, commissioned from Bernini in Rome. When Bernini, that notorious cat-hater, questioned Van Dyck's method, Van Dyck replied, 'If a cat may look at a king, it may also look like a king'.

❖

One wonders if the many *fêtes* that Watteau painted would have been so charming and delicate if he had not employed cats in his early studies. A day in the country was a special treat to them, even if they did have to wear rather confining clothes. Whenever Watteau announced, 'Au bois, mes chats!' they would tumble all over each other in their eagerness to depart, providing one of the familiar sights of 18th-century Paris: Watteau and his cats gambolling to the woods.

❖

This is the only cat study known to have been painted by Hogarth, and the reason is quite obvious. Cats are so innocently amoral that they softened Hogarth's sharply satirical social commentary. Even here, in this scene of unbridled licentiousness, we see only feline pleasure, not moral dissolution.

❖

The Spanish cat has always had a reputation for regal bearing, and Goya clearly took advantage of this to make Charles IV of Spain and his somewhat unprepossessing family look a little more impressive.

Susan Herbert

❖

Although one pseudo-critic has actually had the temerity to suggest that David murdered a cat in the name of realism, this is a base lie. The truth, as I have now been able to determine, is that though David did indeed have great difficulty in getting any of his cats to pose with eyes closed for very long, one of them, Greuze, had a useful habit of closing his eyes in languid bliss when caressed. David accordingly stationed one of his assistants out of sight behind the bath to stroke the cat's back gently while he painted.

❖

À MARAT

DAVID

❖

Not only did Blake rely on his cats for artistic help, he used them for poetic stimulation as well. The cat in this study was also the inspiration for an early draft, 'Cat! cat! burning bright...' The idea was there but Blake clearly found the rythm unsatisfactory, for in the margin he has written 'Find two-syllable feline – kitty?...leopard?...TYGER!'

❖

This study by Courbet was not achieved without some effort. Courbet's cats refused to pose in the company of a dog, even a very tiny one, so Courbet trapped a rat. The poor rat was so terrified by the cats that Courbet had to sedate the animal with absinthe. Even drunk, the rat looks anxious. The moment the study was completed the animal bolted, and a merry chase about Courbet's studio ensued.

❖

❖

Whistler's mother was enraged when by chance she discovered this study. She recognized the cat as an inhabitant of Whistler's studio who had lost an eye in a fight some years before. At last she understood why Whistler had painted her from her 'bad profile'. She was even more enraged when she received a note from John Ruskin informing her that her son had named the cat 'Mother'.

❖

❖

——————————————————

No art movement depended so much on cat
models as the English Pre-Raphaelites.
The members of the Pre-Raphaelite Brotherhood
were all cat-fanciers and Rossetti, Millais and
William Holman Hunt lent their cats to each
other. To what other source can we attribute the
languid, ethereal air that characterizes their
subjects, especially women?

❖

Although a separate study of the influence of cats on Impressionism has been published (*Impressionist Cats*, New York and London, 1992) one has only to look at this snapshot-like impression of reality to understand the innate affinity of cats for this school of painting. Manet, the painter of modern life, was captivated by the way his cats expressed the modern outlook, moving without regret or anticipation from one evanescent moment to another.

❖

Although the gamut of emotions in most cat studies has been limited to those most favoured by cats, in this study, painted shortly before his death, Van Gogh's cat movingly reflects the painter's melancholy.

Among animals, melancholy is mainly an attribute of dogs (who will resort to any cheap bid for affection). A cat's melancholy is the more keenly felt thanks to its sincerity.

❖

Seurat set himself a very hard task in this study. First of all he employed a mouse as a model for a pet. A close look at the foreground figures reveals that the cat is actually lying on the mouse's tail in order to prevent it from escaping. The other difficulty of course is to get cats to spend any time in the water, especially the time required by Seurat's painstaking pointillist technique. Seurat had finally to throw several pounds of sardines into the river. The fact that an artist would go to such lengths for the sake of a study is the clearest demonstration of the importance of cats to individual artists and to the entire history of Western Art.

(OVERLEAF)

Why, when he could have used a mirror for his self-portrait, did Rousseau resort to a cat as a stand-in? Here, the answer is almost too obvious, which is why it has not been seen until now. This painting is *not* a study. Rousseau wanted a picture of his favourite cat, but the cat refused to stand still. So Rousseau set up a mirror, donned this silly costume, and painted his self-portrait as a study for this portrait of his cat.

❖

Susan Herbert